THE ULTIMATE
HUMAN
RESOURCES
ADULT COLORING BOOK

BELONGS TO:

For questions and customer service, email us at
abhiramisummer@gmail.com

IF AT FIRST YOU
Don't succeed
TRY DOING WHAT YOUR
HR Team
Told you
to do
the first
time!

HUMAN RESOURCICORN

Like a normal human resource but more awesome & magical

Made in the USA
Las Vegas, NV
15 September 2023

77596512R10031